Given to the Milton Public Library July 1992, in memory of E. H. "Rooner" Wisbey

YOU'RE ON THE WRONG FOOT AGAIN, CHARLIE BROWN

Charles M. Schulz

TOPPER BOOKS
AN IMPRINT OF PHAROS BOOKS • A SCRIPPS HOWARD COMPANY
NEW YORK

First published in 1987

Paperback edition distributed in the United States by Ballantine Books, a division of Random House, Inc. and in Canada by Random House of Canada, Ltd.

Library of Congress Catalog Card Number: 87-060710
Pharos ISBN: 0-88687-313-4
Ballantine Books ISBN: 0-345-34872-9

Printed in United States of America

Topper Books
An Imprint of Pharos Books
A Scripps Howard Company
200 Park Avenue
New York, NY 10166

10 9 8 7 6 5 4 3 2 1

GRAMMA'S ON THE PHONE..

SHE'S BEEN WONDERING WHY SHE HASN'T HEARD FROM YOU...
© 1985 United Feature Syndicate, Inc.

HI, GRAMMA... IT'S FUNNY THAT YOU SHOULD CALL RIGHT NOW..

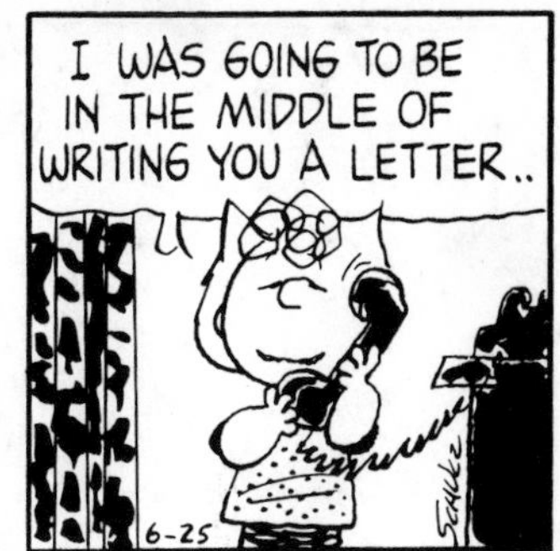
I WAS GOING TO BE IN THE MIDDLE OF WRITING YOU A LETTER..
6-25

AND THEN THIS GIRL SAID TO ME, "GOODBYE, LINUS, I'LL SEE YOU SOMEWHEN!"

"SOMEWHEN"... THAT'S AN OLD COUNTRY EXPRESSION.. IT'S VERY TOUCHING...

REALLY? I THOUGHT I WAS THE ONLY ONE WHO FELT THAT WAY...

6-26

NOT AT ALL..
SNIF!
© 1985 United Feature Syndicate, Inc.

© 1985 United Feature Syndicate, Inc.

6-27
REALLY?

TELL ME MORE..

WOODSTOCK READS SUPPER DISHES!
SCHULZ

PSYCHIATRIC HELP 5¢
THE DOCTOR IS IN

HOW DOES SHE DO BUSINESS WITHOUT ADVERTISING?
SHE HAS THE BEST KIND OF ADVERTISING THERE IS...

ALL RIGHT, WHERE IS EVERYBODY? LET'S GET OVER HERE RIGHT NOW!
6-28

WORD OF MOUTH!
© 1985 United Feature Syndicate, Inc.
SCHULZ

I WOULD HAVE SAID SOMETHING, BUT I WAS AFRAID I'D REGRET IT...

6-29

LIFE IS FULL OF REGRETS, CHARLIE BROWN

NOT IF YOU'RE A DOG... DOGS DON'T HAVE REGRETS

SURE WE DO..I'VE ALWAYS REGRETTED THAT I COULDN'T GROW A BEARD.
© 1985 United Feature Syndicate, Inc.

I'VE BEEN THINKING ABOUT SCHOOL...
7-1
© 1985 United Feature Syndicate, Inc.

I'VE DECIDED TO STUDY REAL HARD THIS YEAR, AND BECOME RICH AND FAMOUS...

IF YOU'LL HELP ME WITH MY HOMEWORK EVERY NIGHT, I'LL SPLIT WITH YOU..

NOT THE RICH.. JUST THE FAMOUS!

PEANUTS®

featuring

"Good ol' Charlie Brown"

by SCHULZ

YOU SHOULD ALWAYS SAVE YOUR TICKET STUB, MARCIE
I DON'T NEED IT..I'M ALREADY IN MY SEAT...

I ALWAYS SAVE MY TICKET STUB IN CASE THEY HAVE A DRAWING FOR A BIG PRIZE...
© 1985 United Feature Syndicate, Inc.
6-30

AT A CONCERT?

I'M THINKING MAYBE THEY'LL GIVE AWAY A VIOLIN..THEY SEEM TO HAVE MORE THAN THEY NEED..
YOU'RE WEIRD, SIR!
SCHULZ

Dear Sweetheart,
I miss you very much.
7-2

Remember how we used to sit in the park eating chocolate chip cookies?

I haven't had a single cookie since you left.

LOVERS LIE!
SCHULZ
© 1985 United Feature Syndicate, Inc.

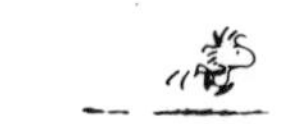

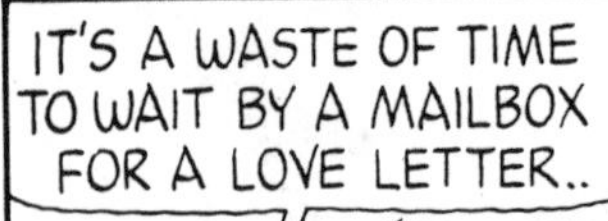
IT'S A WASTE OF TIME TO WAIT BY A MAILBOX FOR A LOVE LETTER..

7-3

IT'LL NEVER COME...

I OUGHT TO KNOW.. I'M AN EXPERT!

WHAT A MISERABLE THING TO BE AN EXPERT AT...
SCHULZ
© 1985 United Feature Syndicate, Inc.

© 1985 United Feature Syndicate, Inc.

7-4

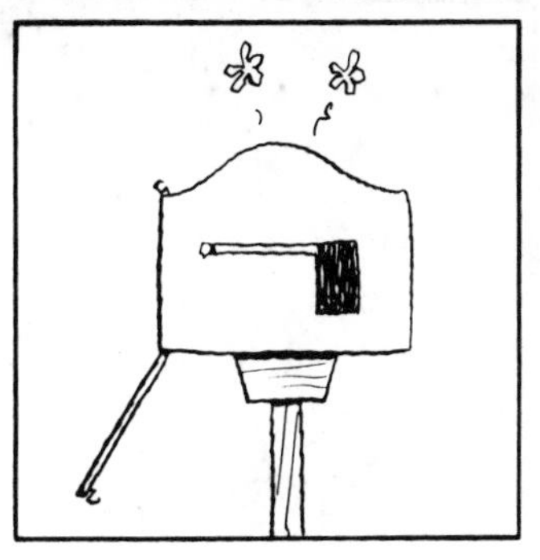

NEVER TRY TO STAND UP INSIDE A MAILBOX!
SCHULZ

HEY, RERUN... MOM'S LOOKING FOR YOU!

I HATE TO TELL YOU, BUT IT'S "B OF THE B" DAY!

OH, NO... NOT "B OF THE B"!
7-5
© 1985 United Feature Syndicate, Inc.

BACK OF THE BIKE DAY!!
SCHULZ

PEANUTS®
featuring
"Good ol' Charlie Brown"
by SCHULZ

HERE'S THE FIERCE JUNGLE ANIMAL PERCHED IN A TREE READY TO POUNCE ON A VICTIM WHO PASSES BELOW..

© 1985 United Feature Syndicate,Inc.

7-7

WHAT CAN YOU EXPECT FROM SOMEONE WHO GRADUATED AT THE BOTTOM OF HIS CLASS AT POUNCE SCHOOL?
SCHULZ

IT'S VERY STRANGE...
7-6
© 1985 United Feature Syndicate, Inc.

SOMETIMES YOU LIE IN BED AT NIGHT, AND YOU DON'T HAVE A SINGLE THING TO WORRY ABOUT...

THAT ALWAYS WORRIES ME!
SCHULZ

I'VE BEEN LISTENING TO THE WEATHER REPORT..

THERE WAS SUPPOSED TO BE A STORM COMING, BUT NOW THEY'RE NOT SURE...
© 1985 United Feature Syndicate, Inc.
7-8

THEY SAID IT WAS "A DAY LATE AND WEAKENING"

SOUNDS A LOT LIKE MYSELF!
SCHULZ

7-9
I'M GOING TO BE IN A DEBATE..

THESE ARE SOME NOTES I'M PREPARING SO I'LL BE READY

"SO? WHO CARES? WHY NOT? FORGET IT!! OH, YEAH? DROP DEAD!"

I THINK YOU'RE READY..
SCHULZ
© 1985 United Feature Syndicate, Inc.

ANOTHER TINY TOTS CONCERT, AND LOOK WHAT THEY'RE PLAYING...

"PETER AND THE WOLF"
AGAIN?

MAYBE THIS TIME WE'LL BE LUCKY...
© 1985 United Feature Syndicate, Inc.
7-10

MAYBE THIS TIME THE WOLF WILL GET HIM!
SCHULZ

I JUST GOT BACK FROM ANOTHER EXCITING TINY TOTS CONCERT..

I HAD A GREAT TIME!

WHAT WAS THE MOST EXCITING PART?
7-11
© 1985 United Feature Syndicate, Inc.

WHEN THE TOWEL RACK FELL OFF THE WALL IN THE LADIES' ROOM!
SCHULZ

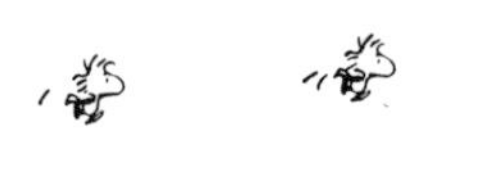

He was a very arrogant cowboy.

He would only ride on pompous grass.

7-12
YOU MEAN PAMPAS GRASS..

I SAID HE WAS ARROGANT, DIDN'T I?
SCHULZ
© 1985 United Feature Syndicate, Inc.

LOOK AT THAT LICENSE PLATE.."HAPPINESS IS BEING SINGLE"

THEN LOOK AT THIS ONE..
© 1985 United Feature Syndicate, Inc.
7-13

"HAPPINESS IS BEING A GRANDPARENT"

IF LICENSE PLATES CAN'T AGREE, HOW CAN THE REST OF US AGREE?
SCHULZ

SOMETHING'S BEEN WORRYING ME...
© 1985 United Feature Syndicate, Inc.

IF WE WERE MARRIED, WOULD YOU CARE IF I PLAYED TENNIS EVERY DAY?
7-15

I WOULDN'T CARE IF YOU PLAYED SHUFFLEBOARD EVERY DAY!

I'M GLAD TO HEAR THAT..
SCHULZ

PEANUTS

featuring "Good ol' Charlie Brown"

by SCHULZ

I CAN HEAR HIM SNORING WAY OUT HERE..

7-14
© 1985 United Feature Syndicate, Inc.

SUPPERTIME!!

PLUNK!

AS THE YEARS GO BY, A GOOD MANAGER GETS TO KNOW HIS PLAYERS..
SCHULZ

WHY DO YOU KEEP TALKING ABOUT US GETTING MARRIED?

IT'S NEVER GOING TO HAPPEN!
7-16

THERE ARE PROBABLY A MILLION GIRLS IN THIS WORLD WHOM I'D RATHER MARRY THAN YOU!

YOU'D GET TIRED OF THEM..
© 1985 United Feature Syndicate, Inc.

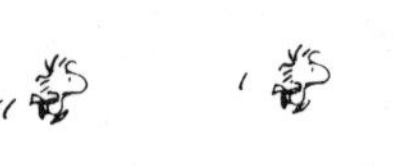

IF YOU'RE AN ATTORNEY, I'D BE INTERESTED IN KNOWING WHAT KIND OF CASES YOU HANDLE...

MAY I SEE ONE OF YOUR CARDS?
© 1985 United Feature Syndicate, Inc.

"ATTORNEY AT LAW.. BANKRUPTCY, TRUSTS, ACCIDENTS, MEDICAL, PROBATE, WILLS..."
7-17

"AND DOG BITES"

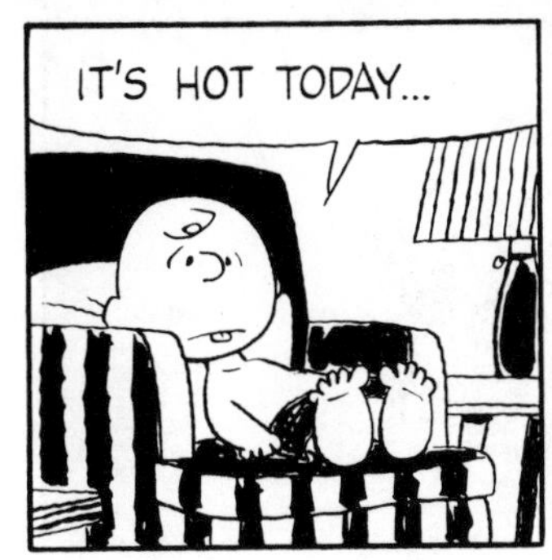
IT'S HOT TODAY...

I WISH WE HAD A POOL OR LIVED NEAR A LAKE..

WELL, THERE'S ONLY ONE THING TO DO...
© 1985 United Feature Syndicate, Inc.

GO DOWN TO THE OL' SWIMMING BUCKET!
SCHULZ
7-18

SO IT'S A HOT DAY... WHY DO YOU HAVE TO SIT IN A BUCKET?

WHY LET THE WHOLE NEIGHBORHOOD KNOW WE DON'T HAVE A POOL?

SOME OF US AREN'T THAT CONCERNED ABOUT OUR IMAGE!

THAT'S TRUE
SCHULZ
© 1985 United Feature Syndicate, Inc.
7-19

PEANUTS®

featuring "Good ol' Charlie Brown"

by SCHULZ

THIS IS OUR FIELD..WE'RE ALREADY THE HOME TEAM

HE'S RIGHT, SIR..THIS IS THEIR FIELD SO THEY'RE ALREADY THE HOME TEAM

OKAY, THEN WE'LL FLIP TO SEE WHO GETS TO BAT LAST!

7-21

THE HOME TEAM ALWAYS BATS LAST..
HE'S RIGHT, SIR..THEY'RE THE HOME TEAM SO THEY GET TO BAT LAST...

MARCIE, WILL YOU STOP TAKING CHUCK'S SIDE ABOUT EVERYTHING?!
RULES ARE RULES, SIR..

WELL, WE HAVE TO FLIP ABOUT SOMETHING!!

ACTUALLY, WE CAN'T FLIP ABOUT ANYTHING BECAUSE WE DON'T HAVE A COIN...
NO PROBLEM, CHUCK... MARCIE HAS A COIN...

NOT ANYMORE!
SCHULZ

HEY, MY SHOELACE IS UNTIED..

BONK!

7-20
© 1985 United Feature Syndicate, Inc.

ARE YOU READY? HERE COMES A NEW EXCUSE!

I ALMOST CAUGHT A FISH!
© 1985 United Feature Syndicate, Inc.

IT WAS ABOUT THIS BIG..

YOU DON'T BELIEVE ME? ALL RIGHT, HOW BIG DO YOU THINK IT WAS?
7-22

COME ON! IT WAS BIGGER THAN THAT!

WHERE HAVE **YOU** BEEN?

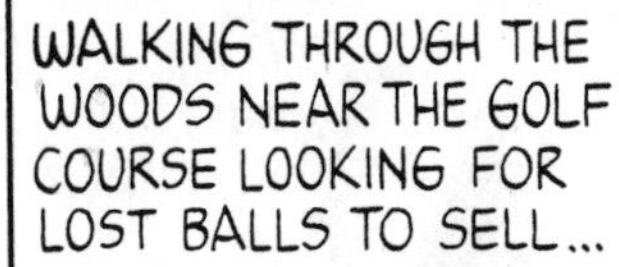
WALKING THROUGH THE WOODS NEAR THE GOLF COURSE LOOKING FOR LOST BALLS TO SELL...

DID YOU MAKE ANY MONEY?
© 1985 United Feature Syndicate, Inc.
7-23

JUST ENOUGH TO PAY FOR THE POISON OAK SHOTS!
SCHULZ

© 1985 United Feature Syndicate, Inc.

POOF!

YOU'RE WELCOME
SCHULZ
7-24

7-25

© 1985 United Feature Syndicate, Inc.

BONK!

SCHULZ

7-26
© 1985 United Feature Syndicate, Inc.

YAWN

?

SCHULZ

7-27

?

© 1985 United Feature Syndicate, Inc.

I DON'T KNOW WHAT IT IS, BUT I CAUGHT IT!
SCHULZ

SUPPERTIME!
7-29
© 1985 United Feature Syndicate, Inc.

JUST IN CASE YOU'RE INTERESTED..

THIS MEAL WAS PROVIDED BY FUNDS FROM THE PRIVATE SECTOR

MY COMPLIMENTS TO THE PRIVATE SECTOR!
SCHULZ

PEANUTS®
featuring
"Good ol' Charlie Brown"
by SCHULZ

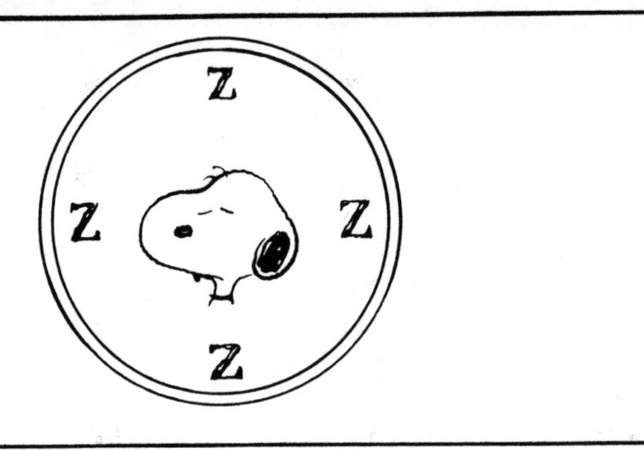

YOU'RE WRONG.. IT ISN'T SUPPERTIME
© 1985 United Feature Syndicate, Inc.

WE HAD A POWER FAILURE LAST NIGHT.. ALL THE CLOCKS ARE OFF

7-28
HOW DO YOU RESET A STOMACH CLOCK?
SCHULZ

JUST EIGHT MORE YEARS!
7-30
© 1985 United Feature Syndicate, Inc.

MY WHOLE LIFE WILL CHANGE..

WHAT HAPPENS IN EIGHT MORE YEARS?

I GET TO HANG AROUND SHOPPING MALLS!

7-31

IT'S A DIFFICULT LANGUAGE..
© 1985 United Feature Syndicate, Inc.

I THINK I CAN BECOME A BETTER PLAYER..

ALL I HAVE TO DO IS PUT MY MIND TO IT..
© 1985 United Feature Syndicate, Inc.

IF YOU START PUTTING YOUR MIND TO IT, WE'RE ALL IN TROUBLE!

A GOOD MANAGER NEVER RESORTS TO SARCASM!
8-1

THERE WILL ALWAYS BE A LACK OF REAL UNDERSTANDING BETWEEN ATHLETES AND OWNERS..
© 1985 United Feature Syndicate, Inc.

..BETWEEN ACTORS AND PRODUCERS...

..BETWEEN WRITERS AND PUBLISHERS...

..BETWEEN DOGS AND PEOPLE..
8-2

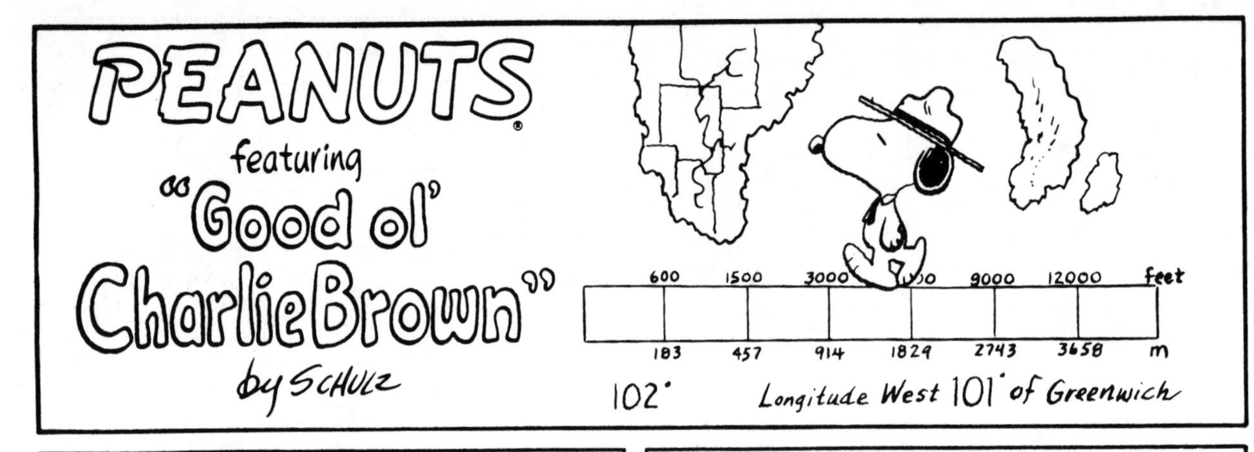
PEANUTS®
featuring
"Good ol' Charlie Brown"
by SCHULZ
600 1500 3000 9000 12000 feet
183 457 914 1829 2743 3658 m
102° Longitude West 101° of Greenwich

OKAY, TROOPS, TODAY WE'RE GOING TO LEARN ABOUT DIRECTIONS AND MAP READING..
8-4

REMEMBER WHAT I TOLD YOU ABOUT THE MOON? YOU CAN ALWAYS TELL WHICH WAY IS WEST BECAUSE THE MOON IS ALWAYS OVER HOLLYWOOD...

IF YOU CAN'T SEE THE MOON, OF COURSE, YOU HAVE TO USE A MAP...

NOW, I WANT YOU TO TAKE THIS MAP, AND SHOW ME WHERE WE ARE RIGHT NOW..

PUT THE MAP SOMEPLACE WHERE YOU CAN ALL SEE IT...

SCHULZ
© 1985 United Feature Syndicate, Inc.

IT SAYS HERE THAT THE TEAM THAT'S IN FIRST PLACE ON THE FOURTH OF JULY USUALLY WINS THE PENNANT

WE WERE IN LAST PLACE ON THE FOURTH OF JULY.. ALSO ON MEMORIAL DAY AND MOTHER'S DAY...

WE'LL PROBABLY BE IN LAST PLACE ON LABOR DAY, COLUMBUS DAY, THANKSGIVING, CHRISTMAS AND YOUR BIRTHDAY!!
8-3

I HATE BEING IN LAST PLACE ON MY BIRTHDAY..
© 1985 United Feature Syndicate, Inc.

WHERE ARE YOU GIRLS GOING?

OVER TO THE SHOPPING MALL..
© 1985 United Feature Syndicate, Inc.

WE'RE "MALLIES"... WE LIKE TO HANG AROUND WITH THE OTHER MALLIES..
8-5

AND THE PUPPIES!

HERE'S SOME CUTE SHOES, SIR
"MALLIES" DON'T BUY THINGS, MARCIE

"MALLIES" JUST HANG AROUND THE SHOPPING MALL ACTING COOL...
© 1985 United Feature Syndicate, Inc.

HI, TIM!
AND WE DON'T WAVE TO THE BOYS!!
8-6

EVERY PLACE I TAKE YOU, MARCIE, YOU EMBARRASS ME!
THESE ARE CUTE SHOES, SIR..

HE'S FOLLOWING ME, SIR..
WHO IS?

A "PUNKER"
© 1985 United Feature Syndicate, Inc.

IGNORE HIM.. BUT THIS IS A PUBLIC SHOPPING MALL SO IF HE'S BOTHERING YOU, REACH UP, AND PUNCH HIM IN THE NOSE...

8-7
HOW ABOUT REACH DOWN?

THAT'S WHAT IT'S ALL ABOUT, RIGHT? HANGING AROUND, RIGHT? BUT YOU KNOW WHAT SHE DID?

8-9

© 1985 United Feature Syndicate, Inc.

HERE, A LETTER FROM SPIKE..

Dear Snoopy,
I think I have found a new way to make some money.
8-10

Wish me luck.
your brother,
Spike
© 1985 United Feature Syndicate, Inc.

AUTHENTIC WESTERN ART

I LIKE TALKING TO MY GRAMPA...

I ASKED HIM IF HE'D LIKE TO BE A YUPPIE..
© 1985 United Feature Syndicate, Inc.

8-12
"I DON'T HAVE TO BE A YUPPIE," HE SAID...

"I'VE ALREADY YUPPED!"

PEANUTS®
featuring
"Good ol' Charlie Brown"
by SCHULZ
DON'T ASK!

DO YOU THINK I'M BEAUTIFUL, CHUCK?
ABSOLUTELY! YOU HAVE AN INNER BEAUTY THAT IS..
© 1985 United Feature Syndicate, Inc.
8-11

NOT INNER BEAUTY, CHUCK! I'M NOT TALKING ABOUT INNER BEAUTY...I'M TALKING ABOUT OUTER BEAUTY!

DO YOU THINK I'M BEAUTIFUL, CHUCK?
I'VE ALWAYS THOUGHT YOU HAD A CUTE WAY ABOUT YOU..YOU KNOW, YOUR EXPRESSIONS, YOUR..

DID I ASK YOU IF I'M CUTE, CHUCK? I DON'T THINK I DID..I ASKED YOU DO YOU THINK I'M BEAUTIFUL?

I JUST REMEMBERED.. THERE'S SOME GOLF ON TV RIGHT NOW!

MY NOSE REMINDED YOU OF A GOLF BALL, HUH, CHUCK? WAS THAT IT, CHUCK?!

ANOTHER "D MINUS"

I KNOW EVERYBODY IN THIS FAMILY HATES ME! I'M GONNA GO WHERE I'M APPRECIATED!

THERE MUST BE A PLACE IN THIS WORLD WHERE I'D BE APPRECIATED..
8-13

© 1985 United Feature Syndicate, Inc.

GIVE ME A HINT..
SCHULZ

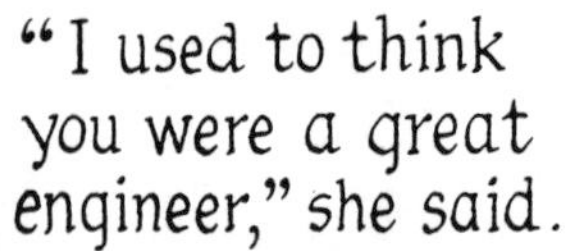
"I used to think you were a great engineer," she said.

8-14

"Once, I even loved you..."

"But you've gotten too big for your bridges."

SCHULZ
© 1985 United Feature Syndicate, Inc.

SCHOOL STARTS IN THREE WEEKS..I HAVE MY CLOTHES ALL LAID OUT...

I EVEN HAVE MY LUNCH MADE..

NOW, I'M GOING OUT TO STAND BY THE BUS STOP...
© 1985 United Feature Syndicate,Inc.

WHAT ARE YOU GOING TO DO OUT THERE?
CRY!
8-15

"DEAR SNOOPY, THIS IS YOUR OL' BROTHER SPIKE WRITING AGAIN FROM THE DESERT"

"TOURISTS SEEM TO LIKE HAND WOVEN BLANKETS"

"ACTUALLY MY WEAVING DIDN'T TURN OUT ALL THAT GOOD.."

© 1985 United Feature Syndicate,Inc.
8-16

PEANUTS
featuring
"Good ol' Charlie Brown"
by SCHULZ

HERE'S THE WORLD FAMOUS EXPLORER LEADING HIS TEAM OF DIVERS TO AN UNDERWATER EXPEDITION...

STAY RIGHT WHERE YOU ARE!! FORGET IT!

Hey!!
WHAT ARE YOU DOING?

8-18
AAUGH!
SSSSSS
© 1985 United Feature Syndicate, Inc.

JACQUES COUSTEAU WOULD NEVER HIDE IN A TREE!
JACQUES COUSTEAU ONLY WORRIES ABOUT SHARKS..
SCHULZ

8-17

© 1985 United Feature Syndicate, Inc.

I HATE TO TELL YOU, BUT THIS ISN'T VERY COMFORTABLE...

THIS IS WORSE..
SCHULZ

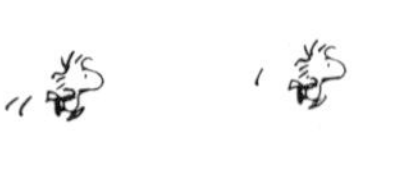

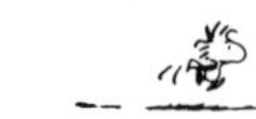

I LOOKED IT UP AT THE CITY HALL...

YOUR GRANDFATHER LED THE GREAT MIGRATION OF '79..
8-19

YOU CAN BE VERY PROUD OF HIM
© 1985 United Feature Syndicate, Inc.

ACTUALLY, I MADE IT ALL UP.. THERE WAS NO MIGRATION OF '79, AND I DON'T EVEN KNOW WHERE THE CITY HALL IS!
SCHULZ

WHAT DID YOU DO WITH THE PICTURE OF ME THAT I GAVE YOU?
© 1985 United Feature Syndicate, Inc.
8-20

I THREW IT AWAY!
WITH YOUR OWN HANDS?

OF COURSE

HE TOUCHED MY PICTURE!
SCHULZ

I KEEP READING THAT OVERPOPULATION IS A PROBLEM..
© 1985 United Feature Syndicate, Inc.

EVEN THE DESERT IS GETTING CROWDED
8-21

BUT I DON'T MIND...

ACTUALLY, I LIKE STANDING IN LINES
SCHULZ

LAST YEAR WHEN I WENT TO SCHOOL, I WAS IN THE WRONG ROOM FOR TWO WEEKS

THEN I GOT IN THE RIGHT ROOM, AND SAT IN THE WRONG DESK..I DIDN'T GET MY LOCKER OPEN THE WHOLE YEAR...

I WAS IN THE BAND FOR THREE DAYS BEFORE I DISCOVERED OUR SCHOOL DOESN'T HAVE A BAND!

I THINK I'LL SIGN UP FOR STAYING HOME..
SCHULZ
© 1985 United Feature Syndicate, Inc.
8-22

WHERE'S MY CADDIE?
8-23

!
OH, HERE YOU ARE
© 1985 United Feature Syndicate, Inc.

IF IT GETS TOO HEAVY, WE CAN ALWAYS TAKE OUT THE TEES..
SCHULZ

HELLO, SCHOOL..
© 1985 United Feature Syndicate, Inc.

ONLY TEN MORE DAYS AND ALL THE KIDS WILL BE BACK!
8-24

SORRY, I DIDN'T MEAN TO STARTLE YOU..
SCHULZ

HEY, YOU'RE SLOWING DOWN!

YOU'RE NOT GETTING OLD, ARE YOU?
8-26

I SURE AM..

I'M FIVE MINUTES OLDER THAN WHEN I STARTED!
SCHULZ
© 1985 United Feature Syndicate, Inc.

PEANUTS®

featuring

"Good ol' Charlie Brown"

by SCHULZ

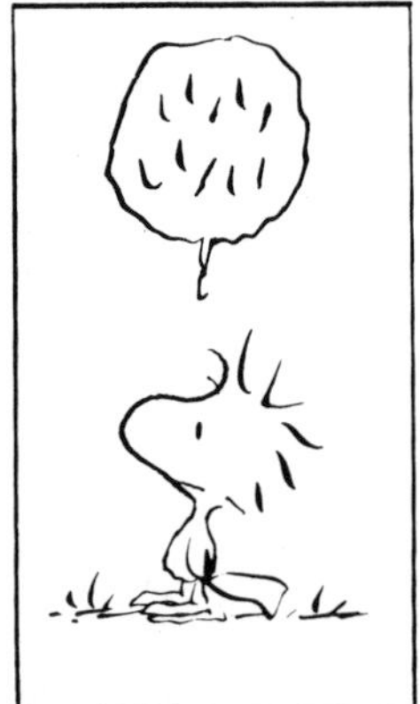

8-25
SCHULZ

THIS IS WHERE WE'LL CATCH THE SCHOOL BUS NEXT WEEK...

I'VE BEEN THINKING ABOUT THIS SCHOOL BUS THING...

I HOPE THAT RIDING ON A BUS WITH A LOT OF SCREAMING KIDS WON'T UPSET YOU...
8/29

NOT A BIT..

I'LL BE SCREAMING THE LOUDEST!
© 1985 United Feature Syndicate, Inc.

WHEN WE RIDE THE BUS TO SCHOOL NEXT WEEK, I'LL PROBABLY SIT WITH MY SWEET BABBOO..

I'M NOT YOUR SWEET BABBOO, AND I'D CRAWL TO SCHOOL ON MY HANDS AND KNEES BEFORE I'D SIT WITH YOU!
8-30

I'M SURE HE'LL INSIST THAT I SIT BY THE WINDOW...

I'LL INSIST THAT YOU SIT ON THE ROOF!!
© 1985 United Feature Syndicate, Inc.
SCHULZ

PEANUTS®

featuring
"Good ol' Charlie Brown"

by SCHULZ

JUST A MINUTE..
I'LL GO SEE...
© 1985 United Feature Syndicate, Inc.

NO, THE CHOCOLATE CHIP COOKIES WEREN'T CALLING YOU..IN FACT, THEY WERE ALL SOUND ASLEEP..
9-1

I WONDER WHAT COOKIES DREAM ABOUT..

IT'S TOO HOT TO SLEEP..
© 1985 United Feature Syndicate, Inc.

WHEN YOU TOSS AND TURN AND CAN'T GET TO SLEEP BECAUSE IT'S JUST TOO HOT...

THERE'S ONLY ONE THING TO DO..

LIE IN YOUR WATER DISH!
8-31
SCHULZ

MARCIE, WHAT WERE THE NAMES OF THOSE BOOKS THE TEACHER WANTED US TO READ THIS SUMMER?

YOU MEAN YOU HAVEN'T READ THEM YET, SIR? SCHOOL STARTS TOMORROW

I HAVE A GOOD EXCUSE..
SCHULZ

THE LIBRARY IS CLOSED TODAY!
© 1985 United Feature Syndicate, Inc.
9-2

HERE'S WHERE WE WAIT FOR THE SCHOOL BUS..

HOW DO I KNOW I'M GOING TO LIKE RIDING ON A SCHOOL BUS?
© 1985 United Feature Syndicate, Inc.

IT'LL BE ALL RIGHT..

DO THEY HAVE IN-FLIGHT MOVIES?
9-3

I'VE CHANGED MY MIND! I DON'T WANT TO RIDE ON THE SCHOOL BUS!!

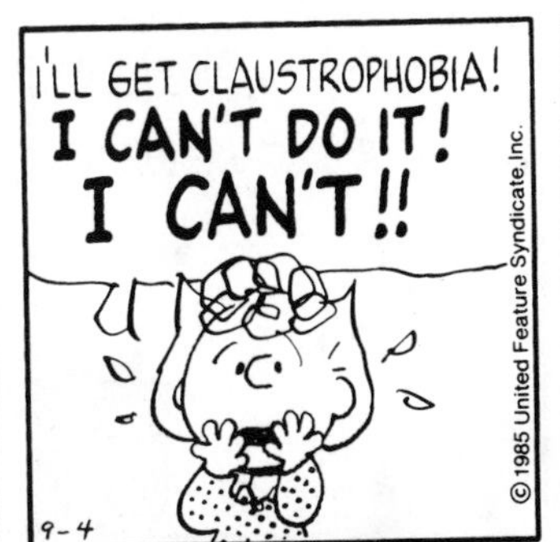
I'LL GET CLAUSTROPHOBIA!
I CAN'T DO IT! I CAN'T!!
© 1985 United Feature Syndicate, Inc.
9-4

WELL, LET'S JUST WALK THEN.. WE HAVE PLENTY OF TIME...

THANK YOU FOR BEING SO UNDERSTANDING, BIG BROTHER..
I DIDN'T WANT TO RIDE ON THE BUS EITHER!

NO, MA'AM, MY SISTER AND I DIDN'T RIDE THE SCHOOL BUS THIS MORNING..NO, MA'AM, WE WALKED...

THE COMPUTER SAID WE WERE ON THE BUS? NO, MA'AM, WE WALKED..
9-5

NO, MA'AM, WE NEVER GOT OFF THE BUS BECAUSE WE WERE NEVER ON THE BUS..WE WALKED...
© 1985 United Feature Syndicate, Inc.

NO, MA'AM.. I NEVER KNOW WHAT'S GOING ON, EITHER..I JUST SIT HERE
SCHULZ

YES, SIR, MR. PRINCIPAL.. I WAS TOLD TO COME SEE YOU...YES, I'M IN SCHOOL TODAY...
9-6

THE COMPUTER SAID I WAS ON THE BUS? AND I NEVER GOT OFF? MY SISTER AND I WALKED, SIR
© 1985 United Feature Syndicate, Inc.

IT WAS A NICE MORNING SO WE WALKED..THE COMPUTER SAID WE WERE ON THE BUS?

NO, SIR, I'M NOT A TROUBLEMAKER
SCHULZ

HEY, CHUCK, I HEARD THEM TALKING ABOUT YOU AT SCHOOL YESTERDAY...

THE COMPUTER SAID YOU WERE SUPPOSED TO BE ON OUR SCHOOL BUS...
© 1985 United Feature Syndicate, Inc.

THAT'S RIDICULOUS! I DON'T EVEN GO TO YOUR SCHOOL!!

WHAT ARE YOU, CHUCK, SOME KIND OF TROUBLEMAKER?
SCHULZ
9-7

HERE COMES THE SCHOOL BUS
© 1985 United Feature Syndicate, Inc.

THE DRIVER SAYS HE CAN'T TAKE YOU..YOUR NAME ISN'T ON THE COMPUTER LIST...

TELL HIM I'M YOUR BROTHER!
9-9

HE WANTS TO KNOW IF YOU'RE SOME KIND OF TROUBLEMAKER..
SCHULZ

YES, MA'AM.. I'M LATE... I DIDN'T PLAN TO BE LATE...
9-10

THE BUS DRIVER SAID I WASN'T ON HIS COMPUTER LIST SO I HAD TO WALK...

I ALSO FORGOT MY LUNCH AND MY HOMEWORK, AND I'M PROBABLY SITTING IN THE WRONG DESK..

HOW DID I KNOW THAT?
SCHULZ

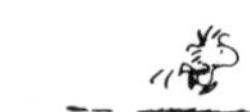

LOOK, MARCIE.. FIVE GOLD CHAINS AND SIX GOLD BRACELETS!

THEY'RE BEAUTIFUL, SIR, BUT AREN'T THEY KIND OF HEAVY?

NOT REALLY
9-11

THEN WHY IS YOUR DESK SINKING?
SCHULZ

SUPPERTIME!

LOOKS PRETTY GOOD, DOESN'T IT?

ACTUALLY, IT LOOKED BETTER FROM A DISTANCE!
© 1985 United Feature Syndicate,Inc.
9-12

9-13
YOU KNOW WHAT, MARCIE?

WE SHOULD BE GRATEFUL THAT WE'RE LIVING AT THIS POINT IN HISTORY

WHICH POINT IS THAT, SIR?

THE GOLDEN AGE OF D-MINUSES!
© 1985 United Feature Syndicate,Inc.

PEANUTS
featuring
"Good ol' Charlie Brown"
by SCHULZ
THIS MAY BE YOUR LAST CHANCE!

DON'T MISS IT! BE THERE!

WAIT! COME BACK! I CAN'T BE THERE! I CAN'T!

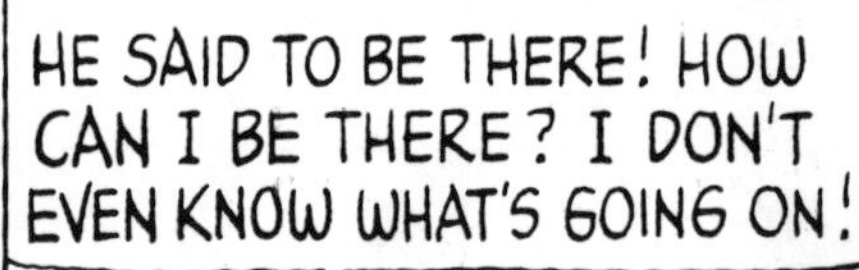
HE SAID TO BE THERE! HOW CAN I BE THERE? I DON'T EVEN KNOW WHAT'S GOING ON!

I CAN'T JUST GO ANYWHERE! WHAT DOES HE EXPECT?!

I DON'T EVEN KNOW WHERE I'M SUPPOSED TO GO!!

LOOK, YOU DON'T HAVE TO DO EVERYTHING THEY TELL YOU ON TV..YOU DON'T HAVE TO BELIEVE ALL THE THINGS THEY SAY..
9-8

YOU'RE KIDDING..

I'M GONNA TRY OUT FOR THE GIRL'S BASKETBALL TEAM

YOU HAVE A LOT TO LEARN...
© 1985 United Feature Syndicate,Inc.

I'VE ALREADY LEARNED SOMETHING...
9-14

YOU DON'T PUT THE KNEEPADS ON OVER YOUR HEAD..
SCHULZ

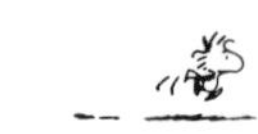

THIS PROGRAM NEEDS YOUR SUPPORT..
9-16 © 1985 United Feature Syndicate,Inc.

WE NEED YOUR DONATIONS...

IF WE DON'T HEAR FROM YOU, WE'LL HAVE TO GO OFF THE AIR...

SO LONG!
SCHULZ

MY REPORT TODAY IS ON HUMAN BEHAVIOR IN OUR SOCIETY...

WE SHALL DISCUSS THE IMPORTANCE OF MARRIAGEMENT..

© 1985 United Feature Syndicate, Inc.
MA'AM?

WHATEVER..
9-17

HAVE YOU EVER THOUGHT THAT MAYBE YOU'RE A LOON?

THEY SAY A LOON HAS A CALL THAT IS VAGUELY FOREBODING...
9-18
© 1985 United Feature Syndicate, Inc.

HA-OO-OO-OO...

TOO FOREBODING!
SCHULZ

PEANUTS
featuring
"Good ol' Charlie Brown"
by SCHULZ
6×2=12
8+6=14

Z

YES, MA'AM, SHE'S ASLEEP... BUT SHE ASKED ME TO TAKE HER CALLS...

9-15
WELL, LET'S SEE...
Z

I'LL SAY, "GEORGE WASHINGTON, NORTH DAKOTA AND IRELAND"

WRONG, HUH? SORRY, MA'AM..
Z
© 1985 United Feature Syndicate, Inc.

SHE CALLED ON YOU WHILE YOU WERE ASLEEP, SIR...

I DIDN'T DO TOO WELL..YOU GOT A "D MINUS"
A "D MINUS"?!

I MAY HAVE TO GET A NEW ANSWERING SERVICE..
SCHULZ

I WONDER IF TEACHERS MAKE A LOT OF MONEY..

WHY DO YOU ASK ?
© 1985 United Feature Syndicate, Inc.

I NOTICE OUR TEACHER JUST BOUGHT A NEW CAR...

I HAVE A FEELING SHE GETS PAID BY THE D-MINUS!
9-19
SCHULZ

It was a dark and stormy night.
9-20

YOU KNOW WHAT'S WRONG WITH YOUR STORIES ?

THEY LACK SUBTLETY
© 1985 United Feature Syndicate, Inc.

It was a sort of dark and kind of stormy night.
SCHULZ

I HATE WAITING FOR SUPPER...

SOMETIMES, IF YOU PRETEND YOU DON'T REALLY CARE, SUPPER COMES FASTER...
9-21

© 1985 United Feature Syndicate, Inc.

IT'S NEVER WORKED YET
SCHULZ

NO, I CAN'T

MY BROTHER IS GOING TO BE GONE THIS AFTERNOON
© 1985 United Feature Syndicate, Inc.

9-23
WHY DO I HAVE TO STAY HOME?

I HAVE TO BEAGLE-SIT!
SCHULZ

PEANUTS®
featuring
"Good ol' Charlie Brown"
by SCHULZ

I'LL COME RUNNING DOWN THE FIELD, AND YOU TRY TO TACKLE ME...

SIGH

9-22

TOUCHDOWN!

I GUESS I WAS WRONG.. YOU'RE TOO SMALL TO PLAY FOOTBALL

MAYBE WE CAN FIND A PLACE FOR YOU IN THE BAND...

SCHULZ

9-24
Z

SHE'S ASLEEP MA'AM..
© 1985 United Feature Syndicate, Inc.

MAYBE WE ALL SHOULD JUST TIPTOE OUT OF THE ROOM, AND LET HER REST, OKAY?

THAT'S ALL RIGHT... IT WAS ONLY A SUGGESTION..
SCHULZ

YES, MA'AM, EVERYONE FEELS SORT OF SLEEPY..

I THINK IT'S STUFFY IN HERE
© 1985 United Feature Syndicate, Inc.

MAYBE WE SHOULD OPEN A FEW WINDOWS

NO, MA'AM.. WE PROMISE NOT TO TRY TO ESCAPE...
SCHULZ
9-25

His was a story that had to be told.
9-26

© 1985 United Feature Syndicate, Inc.

Well, maybe not.

SCHULZ

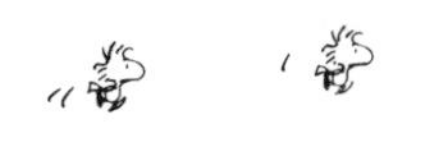

I DREAMED ABOUT THAT LITTLE RED HAIRED GIRL AGAIN LAST NIGHT...

NOW, I'LL BE THINKING ABOUT HER ALL DAY, AND BE DEPRESSED...
© 1985 United Feature Syndicate, Inc.

I THINK I KNOW HOW YOU FEEL, CHARLIE BROWN.. YOU'D LIKE TO CRY, BUT YOU'RE TOO MACHO..
9-27

I **AM** ?!
SCHULZ

PEANUTS®
featuring
"Good ol' Charlie Brown"
by SCHULZ
LOOK AT 'EM..

THEY ALWAYS FASCINATE ME
9-29

SEE HOW THOSE LITTLE BIRDS ARE CHASING THAT BIG BIRD?

HOW CAN THOSE TINY LITTLE BIRDS CHASE THAT BIG BIRD?

YOU'VE ACTUALLY DONE IT YOURSELF, HAVEN'T YOU?

ISN'T IT DANGEROUS?

I GUESS MAYBE IT IS...
SCHULZ

I'M GETTING RESTLESS
10-7 ©1985 United Feature Syndicate, Inc.

I HAVEN'T BEEN INTO TOWN FOR FIVE WEEKS..

TWO WEEKS ?

WELL, IT SEEMS LIKE FIVE WEEKS...
SCHULZ

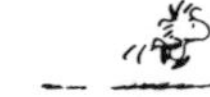

YOU KNOW WHAT YOU COULD BE ?

YOU COULD BE A RAILROAD CROSSING GUARD! YOU COULD STAND BY THE TRACKS, AND WARN PEOPLE THAT A TRAIN WAS COMING...
10-8

WHAT DO YOU THINK ?

YOU NEVER KNOW WHAT THEY REALLY THINK..
SCHULZ ©1985 United Feature Syndicate, Inc.

AH! ANOTHER DAY!
10-9
© 1985 United Feature Syndicate, Inc.

ONE THING ABOUT LIVING IN THE DESERT.. THERE'S ALWAYS SOMETHING EXCITING TO DO...

LIKE RIGHT NOW, FOR INSTANCE...

A ROUSING GAME OF "HAT ON THE CACTUS"!
SCHULZ

I WENT INTO NEEDLES YESTERDAY, AND TALKED TO A PSYCHIATRIST...
10-10
© 1985 United Feature Syndicate, Inc.

I ASKED HIM IF TALKING TO A CACTUS WAS A SIGN I WAS GOING CRAZY...

"NO," HE SAID, "ONLY IF THE CACTUS STARTS TO TALK BACK!"

PLEASE DON'T SAY ANYTHING..
SCHULZ

THE MEETING OF THE CACTUS CLUB WILL COME TO ORDER...
10-11 © 1985 United Feature Syndicate, Inc.

THE SECRETARY WILL READ THE MINUTES OF THE LAST MEETING...

"A SUGGESTION WAS MADE THAT WE PURCHASE A COMPUTER TO KEEP TRACK OF OUR MEMBERSHIP"

"AFTER THE LAUGHTER DIED DOWN, WE HAD REFRESHMENTS"
SCHULZ

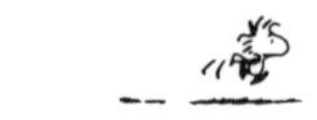

LIVING IN THE DESERT ISN'T ALL BAD...
10-12 © 1985 United Feature Syndicate, Inc.

THERE'S BEAUTIFUL SCENERY...

AND GOOD CONVERSATION..

HI, ROCK!
SCHULZ

PIGPEN, EVERY LITTLE MOVE YOU MAKE RAISES A CLOUD OF DUST!

I'M SORRY.. I CAN'T HELP IT

© 1985 United Feature Syndicate, Inc.
10-1

STOP BLINKING YOUR EYES!
SCHULZ

RELATIVELY TRUE! MARGINALLY FALSE! APPARENTLY TRUE!
© 1985 United Feature Syndicate, Inc.
10-2

REASONABLY FALSE! BORDERINGLY TRUE!

AND, FORTUNATELY FOR ALL OF US, FALSE!!

YOU'RE WEIRD, SIR
SCHULZ

PEANUTS®
featuring
"Good ol' Charlie Brown"
by SCHULZ

I WAITED FOR THE "WALK" SIGN TO COME ON..

BUT AS SOON AS I TOOK SIX STEPS, IT SAID "DON'T WALK" SO I RAN BACK TO THE CURB!

THEN I WAITED 'TIL IT SAID "WALK" AGAIN, BUT AS SOON AS I TOOK SIX STEPS, IT SAID "DON'T WALK"
10-6

SO I RAN BACK TO THE CURB!

THEN IT SAID "WALK" SO I TRIED IT AGAIN..

THEN IT SAID "DON'T WALK" SO I RAN BACK TO THE CURB...

ASK MOM TO COME DOWN HERE WITH THE CAR, WILL YOU? I CAN'T GET HOME!
SCHULZ

© 1985 United Feature Syndicate, Inc.
9-28

DO KITES HAVE TO HAVE TAILS?

OF COURSE

HOW ELSE COULD THEY TELL YOU WHEN THEY'RE HAPPY?
SCHULZ

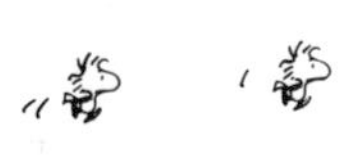

boot!
9-30

© 1985 United Feature Syndicate, Inc.

BONK!

WHAT ARE **YOU** LOOKING AT?!
SCHULZ

NOT A BAD STORY

THIS ONE SECTION BOTHERS ME, THOUGH...

I THINK YOU SHOULD CROSS OUT THE PART WHERE YOUR HERO TAKES A NAP...
10-3

Z-Z-Z-Z-Z-
SCHULZ
© 1985 United Feature Syndicate, Inc.

I'VE HEARD THAT YOUR ADVICE ISN'T ANY GOOD...
THE DOCTOR IS IN

THEY SAY IT'S JUST "POP PSYCHOLOGY"... SO I HAVE TO ASK YOU SOMETHING...
10-4
© 1985 United Feature Syndicate, Inc.

WHAT KIND OF PROBLEMS CAN YOU SOLVE WITH POP PSYCHOLOGY ?
THE DOCTOR

POP PROBLEMS!
SCHULZ
THE DOCTOR IS IN

PEANUTS
featuring
"Good ol' Charlie Brown"
by SCHULZ
BEWARE OF THE BAIT

10-13

HEE
HEE
HEE
HEE
SCHULZ

I'VE COMPILED THE STATISTICS ON OUR BASEBALL TEAM FOR LAST SEASON...
10-5

IN TWELVE GAMES, WE ALMOST SCORED A RUN.. IN NINE GAMES, THE OTHER TEAM ALMOST DIDN'T SCORE BEFORE THE FIRST OUT

IN RIGHT FIELD, LUCY ALMOST CAUGHT THREE BALLS AND ONCE ALMOST MADE THE RIGHT PLAY..

WE LED THE LEAGUE IN "ALMOSTS," CHARLIE BROWN!
SCHULZ
© 1985 United Feature Syndicate, Inc.

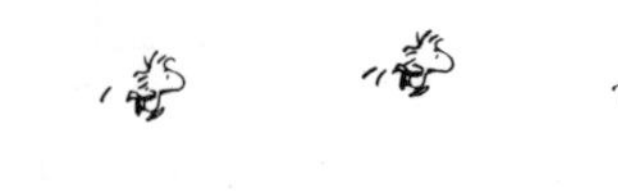

YES, MA'AM..I WALKED TO SCHOOL IN THE RAIN...
© 1985 United Feature Syndicate, Inc.

I HAVE A SAMPLE BOTTLE OF SHAMPOO HERE IN MY PURSE, SIR...

?

MARCIE!!

DON'T LOOK AT ME LIKE THAT, MA'AM; LAST YEAR YOU SAID NOTHING WOULD EVER SURPRISE YOU AGAIN!

SCHULZ
10-14

I KNOW THE ANSWER! IT WAS HENRY VEE!

HENRY VEE WAS KING OF ENGLAND IN 1413!
10-15

HENRY V, SIR... NOT HENRY VEE..
© 1985 United Feature Syndicate, Inc.

AND ANOTHER PUPIL SINKS SLOWLY BENEATH HER DESK...

I'M OUR SCHOOL BOOK REVIEWER

I NEED TO CHECK YOUR NOVEL TO SEE IF IT'S SUITABLE FOR OUR SCHOOL LIBRARY...

"Rats!" cried the hero.
10-16
© 1985 United Feature Syndicate, Inc.

"CONTAINS MILD PROFANITY.."

PEANUTS®

featuring

"Good ol' Charlie Brown"

by SCHULZ

REALLY? I'LL GO CHECK..
© 1985 United Feature Syndicate, Inc.
10-20

♪ ♫

YOU WERE RIGHT... THE LID WAS OFF THE JAR

NO ONE CAN SLEEP WITH A BUNCH OF CHOCOLATE CHIP COOKIES SINGING ALL NIGHT..
SCHULZ

THIS IS MY REPORT ON HALLEY'S COMET WHICH WILL BE COMING BY THE EARTH SOON...

UNFORTUNATELY, IT WILL BE DOWN NEAR THE HORIZON, AND WE WON'T BE ABLE TO SEE IT VERY WELL...
10-17

ACTUALLY, YOU'LL BE ABLE TO SEE IT MUCH BETTER ON TV SOMETIME IN THE MONTH OF MARCH

UNLESS, OF COURSE, YOU'RE WATCHING SATURDAY MORNING CARTOONS..
© 1985 United Feature Syndicate, Inc.
SCHULZ

HALLEY'S COMET IS ACTUALLY A LARGE CHUNK OF DIRTY ICE...

THE NEXT TIME IT PASSES OUR EARTH WILL BE IN THE YEAR 2062...

10-18

OF COURSE, WE'LL ALL BE EIGHTY YEARS OLD WHEN THAT HAPPENS...

EXCEPT FOR YOU, MA'AM..
© 1985 United Feature Syndicate, Inc.
SCHULZ

THIS PROGRAM IS CALLED "GREAT IDEAS OF WESTERN MAN"
© 1985 United Feature Syndicate, Inc.

WHY DON'T YOU GET UP OUT OF THAT BEANBAG, AND LET ME LIE THERE?
10-19

NOW, WHY DON'T YOU GO INTO THE KITCHEN, AND GET ME A DISH OF ICE CREAM?

"GREAT IDEAS OF WESTERN WOMAN!"
SCHULZ

IN 1927, CHARLES LINDBERGH MADE THE FIRST NONSTOP SOLO FLIGHT FROM NEW YORK TO PARIS..

HE WAS KNOWN AS "THE LONE EAGLE"

WHO ELSE DO YOU THINK COULD HAVE MADE A FLIGHT LIKE THAT?

"THE LONE BEAGLE"
SCHULZ
© 1985 United Feature Syndicate, Inc.
10-21

HERE'S THE "LONE BEAGLE" MAKING HIS HISTORIC FLIGHT ACROSS THE ATLANTIC TO PARIS...

FAR BELOW HE CAN SEE THE DARK WATERS OF THE ATLANTIC...

YOUR WATER DISH IS GETTING LOW..I THINK I'D BETTER FILL IT...

THE DARK WATERS OF THE ATLANTIC DISAPPEAR BENEATH HIS PLANE...

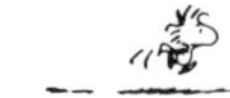

HERE'S THE "LONE BEAGLE" LANDING HIS PLANE IN PARIS AFTER A HISTORIC FLIGHT ACROSS THE ATLANTIC!

WITH CONSUMMATE SKILL HE SETS THE WHEELS DOWN ON THE UNEVEN FIELD...

BONJOUR, MONSIEUR

THOUSANDS OF SCREAMING ADMIRING FRENCH GIRLS SURROUND HIS PLANE...
WHEE!

THIS IS YOUR REPORTER INTERVIEWING THE FAMOUS "LONE BEAGLE" AFTER HIS FLIGHT ACROSS THE ATLANTIC
10-24

HOW DID YOU FEEL AFTER YOU LANDED? HOW DID YOU FEEL WHEN YOU TOOK OFF? HOW DO YOU FEEL?

IF YOU WERE A TREE, WHAT KIND OF TREE WOULD YOU LIKE TO BE? HOW DOES IT FEEL TO HAVE FEELINGS? HOW DO YOU FEEL?

boot!
BACK TO OUR STUDIO!

HERE'S THE "LONE BEAGLE" BACK HOME AFTER HIS HISTORIC FLIGHT FROM NEW YORK TO PARIS...

RIDING THROUGH THE CITY, HE IS GREETED BY CHEERING THRONGS IN A HUGE TICKER TAPE PARADE...
10-25

A ONE TICKER TAPE PARADE..
SCHULZ

PEANUTS
featuring
"Good ol' Charlie Brown"
by SCHULZ
RING

GOOD MORNING, SIR..MY NAME IS LINUS VAN PELT... HALLOWEEN WILL SOON BE HERE, AND I'D LIKE TO TELL YOU A LITTLE ABOUT THE "GREAT PUMPKIN"

PUMPKINS? NO, WE AIN'T BOUGHT ANY PUMPKINS YET..

WELL, WHAT I REALLY MEANT WAS..
HEY, ESTELLE, ARE WE GONNA BUY ANY PUMPKINS THIS YEAR? YEAH, HALLOWEEN IS COMIN'!
10-27

BUT I'M NOT..
THERE'S A KID HERE SELLING PUMPKINS...

NO, I JUST WANT TO TELL YOU ABOUT THE "GREAT PUMPKIN," AND HOW HE..
OKAY, IF THEY'RE GREAT, I'LL ORDER A COUPLE..HEY, ESTELLE, BRING MY WALLET, WILL YOU?

JUST A MINUTE, KID... I'LL GIVE YOU FIVE BUCKS, AN' YOU CAN DELIVER THE PUMPKINS LATER, OKAY?

I NEVER REALIZED EVANGELISM COULD BE SO PROFITABLE!
SCHULZ

THERE GOES YOUR LITTLE BROTHER RIDING ON THE BACK OF YOUR MOM'S BICYCLE

I SEE HE'S FINALLY WEARING A HELMET...
10-26

BUT I'M NOT SURE HE LIKES IT..
© 1985 United Feature Syndicate, Inc.

PEOPLE CONFUSE ME WITH WAYNE GRETZKY!
SCHULZ

I MISSED SCHOOL YESTERDAY BECAUSE I HAD A COLD...

THERE MUST BE SOMETHING GOING AROUND.. LOTS OF KIDS HAVE BEEN GETTING COLDS...
10-28

MINE WAS A LOT WORSE, THOUGH...
WHY?
SCHULZ

BECAUSE IT HAPPENED TO ME!
© 1985 United Feature Syndicate, Inc.

© 1985 United Feature Syndicate, Inc.
10-29

bump!

I DON'T KNOW, OFFICER... IT WAS EITHER A BULLDOZER, A ZAMBONI OR A 747!
SCHULZ

MY GRAMPA IS A "FREQUENT FLIER" SO YESTERDAY HE WENT TO THE AIRPORT...
© 1985 United Feature Syndicate, Inc.

THE LADY BEHIND THE TICKET COUNTER SAID, "OH, YOU'VE ALREADY FLOWN A HUNDRED THOUSAND MILES"

"YOU DON'T HAVE TO MAKE THIS TRIP," SHE SAID.. "YOU CAN GO HOME!" SO HE WENT HOME!
10-30

YOUR WHOLE FAMILY'S WEIRD, MARCIE..
SCHULZ

PEANUTS
featuring
"Good ol' Charlie Brown"
by SCHULZ

IT'S A LETTER FROM YOUR BROTHER SPIKE..

"DEAR SNOOPY, SOMETHING WONDERFUL JUST HAPPENED..."

"A MAN CAME BY HERE, AND OFFERED TO SELL ME A MAGIC CAPE.."

"HE TOLD ME IF I WORE THIS MAGIC CAPE, I'D BE TRANSPORTED TO A LAND OF PARADISE!"

"HE SAID THE CAPE WAS ON SALE... NOT WANTING TO MISS SUCH A BARGAIN, I GAVE HIM MY ONLY DOLLAR..."

"SO BY THE TIME YOU GET THIS LETTER, I'LL BE LIVING IN PARADISE"
11-3

THEN AGAIN, MAYBE I'VE BEEN HAD...
SCHULZ

10-31

RING!
© 1985 United Feature Syndicate, Inc.

I FORGOT THE WORDS!
SCHULZ

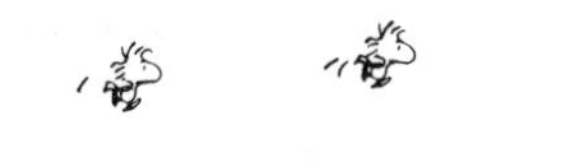

11-1
OH, NO!

WHAT'S THAT HE'S GOT WITH HIM?
© 1985 United Feature Syndicate, Inc.

I CAN'T BELIEVE IT...

A BEAGLE BLASTER!
SCHULZ

I SEE IT! I SEE IT!
© 1985 United Feature Syndicate, Inc.

I SEE HALLEY'S COMET!
11-4

THAT'S NOT HALLEY'S COMET.. THAT'S A STREET LIGHT...

I SEE IT! I SEE IT! I SEE HALLEY'S STREET LIGHT!!
SCHULZ

THERE IT IS! THERE'S HALLEY'S COMET, AND THERE'S ANOTHER ONE RIGHT BESIDE IT!

THOSE AREN'T COMETS... THOSE ARE THE HEADLIGHTS ON A CAR..

11-5
REALLY? THAT'S A SHAME

ASTRONOMERS ALL OVER THE WORLD WILL BE FOOLED AGAIN!
SCHULZ
© 1985 United Feature Syndicate, Inc.

I'LL HOLD YOU UP, AND WHEN HALLEY'S COMET COMES BY, YOU BARK...
11-6

WOOF!

WHERE? WHERE?
© 1985 United Feature Syndicate, Inc.

SORRY, IT WAS JUST THE MOON REFLECTING OFF MY SUPPER DISH..
SCHULZ

LIFT ME HIGHER.. WHEN HALLEY'S COMET COMES BY, I WANT TO SEE IT...

11-7

OKAY, NOW HAND ME THE BINOCULARS
© 1985 United Feature Syndicate, Inc.

AAUGH!

STUPID BEAGLE!!
SCHULZ

I HOPE YOU REALIZE THAT HALLEY'S COMET WON'T BE VISIBLE FOR AT LEAST ANOTHER MONTH...
11-8

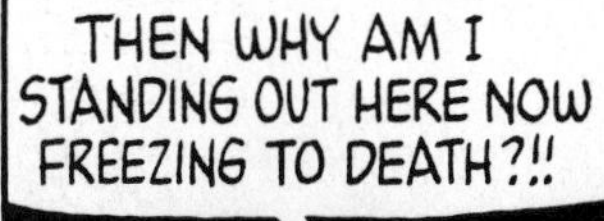

THEN WHY AM I STANDING OUT HERE NOW FREEZING TO DEATH?!!
© 1985 United Feature Syndicate, Inc.

NOBODY TELLS ME ANYTHING!

NOBODY TELLS ME ANYTHING EITHER, BUT I LIKE IT THAT WAY..
SCHULZ

HOW COULD YOU NOT KNOW WHEN HALLEY'S COMET IS COMING?

YOU DID A REPORT ON IT IN SCHOOL JUST TWO WEEKS AGO..
11-9

YOU READ THE REPORT TO THE WHOLE CLASS!

I ONLY READ THE REPORT.. I DIDN'T LISTEN TO IT...
SCHULZ
© 1985 United Feature Syndicate, Inc.

PEANUTS®
featuring
"Good ol' Charlie Brown"
by SCHULZ

His bus left at midnite.

THAT'S NOT HOW YOU SPELL "MIDNIGHT"

AH, YOU RECOGNIZED THE WORD, THOUGH, DIDN'T YOU?

11-10
AND LOOK WHAT I SAVED... I SAVED A "G" AND AN "H"!
© 1985 United Feature Syndicate, Inc.

NOW, IF I EVER NEED A "G" OR AN "H," I'LL BE READY...

WHERE ARE YOU GOING TO USE THE "G" AND "H" YOU SAVED?

"Wright when you get there!" said his mother.

SCHULZ

YOU THINK LIFE DOWN HERE IS GOING TO BE BETTER, DON'T YOU?

WELL, IT ISN'T
© 1985 United Feature Syndicate, Inc.

WHERE ARE YOU GOING TO GO? WHERE ARE YOU GOING TO STAY?

"WITH RELATIVES"?
SCHULZ
11-2

TODAY IS VETERANS DAY.. I ALWAYS GET TOGETHER WITH OL' BILL MAULDIN ON VETERANS DAY, AND QUAFF A FEW ROOT BEERS...

OL' BILL AND I CAN REALLY PUT 'EM AWAY..

HEY, BILL, AS LONG AS YOU'RE UP, ORDER A COUPLE MORE! I'M PAYIN'!
11-11

BUT TELL 'IM WE WANT MORE ICE CREAM IN THE NEXT ONES!
SCHULZ
© 1985 United Feature Syndicate, Inc.

FOURTEEN?

TWENTY-TWO? SIXTY-THREE?

SORRY, MA'AM..

I THINK MY MATH BOOK HAS A CHILD-RESISTANT CAP!
SCHULZ
11-12

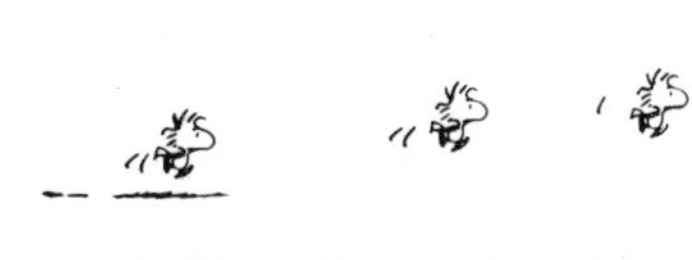

HI!
11-13

PAY ATTENTION TO ME!!
SCHULZ

TO ME, BREAKFAST IS THE BEST TIME OF DAY
11-14

EVEN WHEN YOU LIVE ALONE ON THE DESERT

©1985 United Feature Syndicate,Inc.

EXCEPT WHEN A TUMBLEWEED ROLLS THROUGH YOUR PANCAKES..
SCHULZ

ASK YOUR DAD IF HE WANTS ME TO SHOVEL YOUR WALK..

HE SAID WHY SHOULD HE PAY YOU WHEN HE CAN DO IT HIMSELF?
©1985 United Feature Syndicate,Inc.

BECAUSE IF HE DOES IT HIMSELF, HE'S LIABLE TO HAVE A HEART ATTACK AND NEED BYPASS SURGERY...
11-15
WHO WRITES YOUR COMMERCIALS?
SCHULZ

GOOD MORNING, EVERYBODY!

IS THERE ANYTHING I CAN DO AROUND THE HOUSE TODAY TO JUSTIFY MY EXISTENCE?

11-16
YOU COULD LEAVE..
© 1985 United Feature Syndicate, Inc.

THE MOUTH IS QUICKER THAN THE BRAIN!
SCHULZ

I GAVE MY REPORT IN SCHOOL TODAY...

AT THE END I SAID, "THIS REPORT WAS WRITTEN ON RECYCLED PAPER..NO TREES WERE DESTROYED TO MAKE THIS REPORT"

DID THE TEACHER APPRECIATE IT?
© 1985 United Feature Syndicate, Inc.

11-18
NO, BUT THE TREES DID!
SCHULZ

PEANUTS®
featuring
"Good ol' Charlie Brown"
by SCHULZ

OKAY, TROOPS.. I THINK WE'VE HIKED FAR ENOUGH...

IT'S A LONG WAY BACK... WE'LL BE LUCKY IF WE GET HOME BY DARK..

WE HAVE TO GO OVER THOSE HILLS, DOWN THROUGH THAT VALLEY, ACROSS THAT STREAM AND THROUGH THAT FOREST...

11-17
ARE THERE ANY QUESTIONS?

"WHY DON'T WE JUST FLY HOME?"

CHEATERS! CHEATERS!
SCHULZ

WOULD YOU LIKE TO BUY A CHRISTMAS WREATH?
© 1985 United Feature Syndicate, Inc.

IT'S NOT EVEN THANKSGIVING YET!
11-19

BY THE TIME CHRISTMAS COMES, ALL THE NEEDLES WILL BE FALLING OFF...

DON'T HANG IT NEAR THE TURKEY..

WOULD YOU LIKE TO BUY A CHRISTMAS WREATH?

IT ISN'T EVEN THANKSGIVING YET!
11-20

© 1985 United Feature Syndicate, Inc.

WOULD YOU LIKE TO BUY A THANKSGIVING WREATH?

WOULD YOU LIKE TO BUY A CHRISTMAS WREATH?
11-21

DO YOU KNOW WHAT YOU'RE DOING?
© 1985 United Feature Syndicate, Inc.

DON'T YOU REALIZE YOU'RE ADDING TO THE OVERCOMMERCIALIZING OF CHRISTMAS?

NOT 'TIL I SELL ONE!
SCHULZ

GOOD MORNING! THIS IS A CHRISTMAS WREATH, AND...
11-22

THANK YOU! I LOVE SAMPLES!
SLAM!

I GIVE UP! I CAN'T IMAGINE ANYONE ELSE HAVING AS MUCH TROUBLE AS I DO SELLING CHRISTMAS WREATHS...

© 1985 United Feature Syndicate, Inc.
SCHULZ

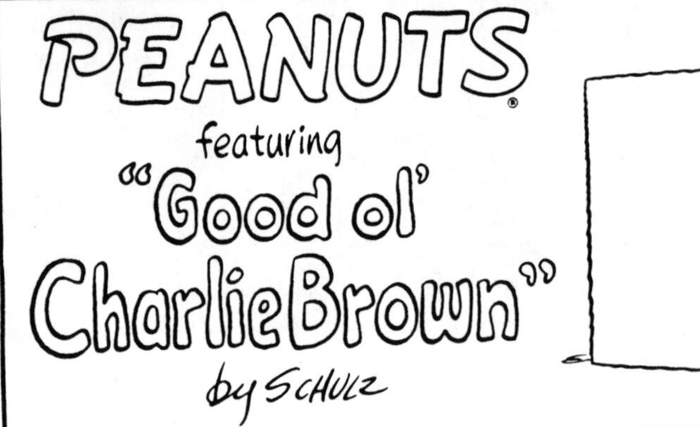
PEANUTS®
featuring
"Good ol' Charlie Brown"
by SCHULZ

I AGREE.. THEY DO SOME STRANGE THINGS...
11-24

YEARS AGO THEY USED TO KILL LAMBS! "SACRIFICE" THEY CALLED IT.. HA!

AND NOW IT'S THANKSGIVING AGAIN..YOU KNOW HOW THEY SHOW THANKS, DON'T YOU? THEY EAT A BIRD! CAN YOU IMAGINE? THEY EAT A BIRD!

WHAT A WAY TO SHOW THANKS! AS LONG AS I LIVE, I'LL NEVER UNDERSTAND THEM!

boot!

WHAT WAS THAT ALL ABOUT?
SCHULZ

WATCHING A FOOTBALL GAME, I SEE...

WHY DOES SOMEONE ALWAYS HANG A SIGN OVER THE RAILING THAT SAYS, "JOHN 3:16"?
© 1985 United Feature Syndicate, Inc.
11-23

IT'S A SCRIPTURAL REFERENCE
REALLY? THEN I WAS WRONG...

I ALWAYS THOUGHT IT HAD SOMETHING TO DO WITH JOHN MADDEN..
SCHULZ

ARE YOU GOING TO HAVE A BIG THANKSGIVING DINNER, CHARLIE BROWN?

I SUPPOSE SO.. BIG DINNERS DON'T REALLY INTEREST ME...

I'VE NEVER THOUGHT THAT MUCH ABOUT EATING...

YOU DO WHEN YOUR DISH IS EMPTY!
SCHULZ
11-28
© 1985 United Feature Syndicate, Inc.

Z
Z
© 1985 United Feature Syndicate, Inc.

11-25
Z
Z

KLUNK!!

WE'RE AWAKE!
SCHULZ

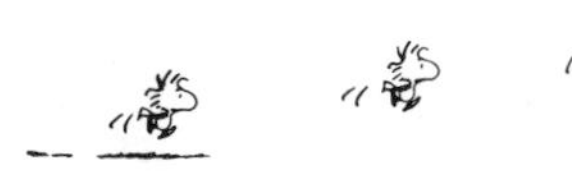

NICE GOING, MARCIE.. WE BOTH FALL ASLEEP IN CLASS..AND NOW WE HAVE TO REPORT TO THE PRINCIPAL'S OFFICE...

11-26
I COULDN'T STAY AWAKE, SIR..
© 1985 United Feature Syndicate, Inc.

PRINCIPAL'S OFFICE

MAYBE WE SHOULDN'T WAKE HIM UP..
Z
SCHULZ

TODAY, MARCIE, I'M GONNA TEACH YOU HOW TO BLOCK A PUNT...

OKAY, YOU PUNT IT, AND I'LL COME RUNNING IN TO BLOCK IT!
© 1985 United Feature Syndicate, Inc.

OOF!

11-27
SOMEHOW, SIR, LEARNING THAT DOESN'T REALLY INTEREST ME..
SCHULZ

THIS TIME, MARCIE, I'LL PUNT, AND YOU BE THE ONE WHO TRIES TO BLOCK IT...

READY, SIR? HERE I COME!
© 1985 United Feature Syndicate, Inc.
11-29

THUMP!

YOUR STYLE, MARCIE, LEAVES A LOT TO BE DESIRED!
SCHULZ

KICK THE BALL, MARCIE!

IT'LL HATE ME, SIR..

FOOTBALLS DON'T HATE, MARCIE!

HOW NICE OF YOU..

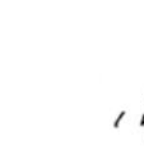

WHAT HAPPENED? DID I MISS ANYTHING?

HE MADE A TOUCHDOWN, AND THE GREAT CROWD GAVE HIM A BIG HAND...

OR MAYBE THE BIG CROWD GAVE HIM A GREAT HAND...I DON'T KNOW..

WHATEVER.. WHO CARES?

PEANUTS
featuring
"Good ol' Charlie Brown"
by SCHULZ

THERE'S THE TELEPHONE..I'D GIVE ANYTHING TO HAVE THE NERVE TO CALL THAT LITTLE RED HAIRED GIRL...

WHY DON'T YOU JUST DO IT?
BECAUSE I KNOW SHE WOULDN'T WANT TO TALK TO ME...

THAT'S RIDICULOUS, CHARLIE BROWN.. WE SEE HER IN SCHOOL EVERY DAY... SHE'S A VERY NICE PERSON!

SHE'LL TALK TO YOU..I KNOW SHE WILL...
I DOUBT IT..I'D JUST BE MAKING A FOOL OF MYSELF
12-1

GO AHEAD.. DO IT! CALL HER!
ALL RIGHT, BUT I'LL BET SHE WON'T EVEN GIVE ME THE TIME OF DAY...

WELL, WHAT HAPPENED?
SHE SAID IT WAS FOUR O'CLOCK!
SCHULZ

Dear Santa Claus,
I saw a recent picture of you in a magazine.
12-3

You look fatter than ever.
© 1985 United Feature Syndicate, Inc.

I know how you usually fly through the air with your reindeer and sleigh.

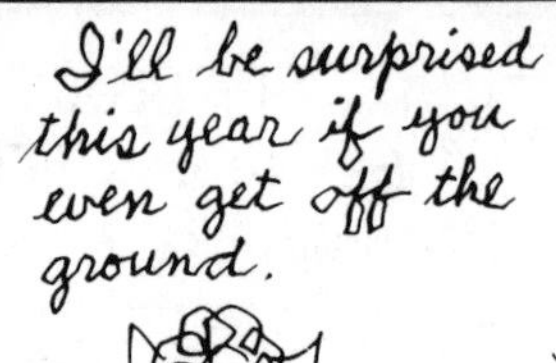
I'll be surprised this year if you even get off the ground.

SCHULZ

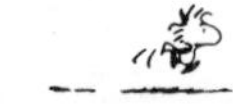

WHAT ARE WE GOING TO HEAR TODAY, MARCIE?

12-18

HANDEL'S "MESSIAH"

THE MOST EXCITING PART IS WHEN THEY GET TO THE "HALLELUJAH CHORUS," AND EVERYONE STANDS...

STANDING IS EXCITING?
© 1985 United Feature Syndicate, Inc.
SCHULZ

IT'S THE "HALLELUJAH CHORUS," SIR..EVERYONE IS STANDING UP...

THEY'RE WHAT?
STANDING UP...

YIPE!!
© 1985 United Feature Syndicate, Inc.
12-19

EVERYWHERE WE GO, MARCIE, YOU EMBARRASS ME!
SCHULZ

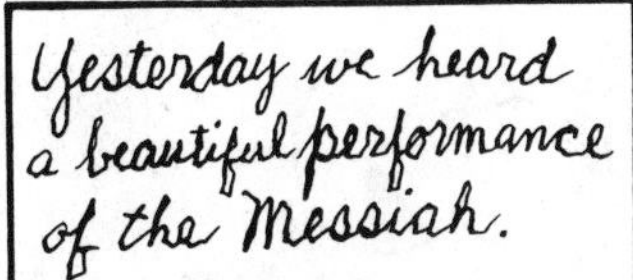
Yesterday we heard a beautiful performance of the Messiah.

12-20

WHAT WAS HANDEL'S FIRST NAME, MARCIE?

I'M ASHAMED TO ADMIT I DON'T KNOW
I'LL JUST HAVE TO GUESS..

It was written by Joe Handel.
SCHULZ
© 1985 United Feature Syndicate, Inc.

PEANUTS®
featuring
"Good ol' Charlie Brown"
by SCHULZ

TOUCHDOWN!

GIMME FIVE!

12-8
WHAP!

HOW DO YOU "UNFIVE"?
SCHULZ

YOU KNOW WHY I DON'T WANT YOU TO BUY ME ANYTHING FOR CHRISTMAS THIS YEAR?

BECAUSE I KNOW YOU HATE ME!
© 1985 United Feature Syndicate, Inc.

12-5
I'VE NEVER SAID I HATE YOU...

THEN BUY ME SOMETHING!!

Dear Grandma,
How have you been?
12-6
© 1985 United Feature Syndicate, Inc.

I hope you have a very merry

mas

WISH HER A MERRY SMUDGMAS FOR ME, TOO!
SCHULZ

LOOK! LOOK AT THIS PICTURE OF SANTA CLAUS! DON'T TELL ME HE ISN'T OVERWEIGHT!

WHAT IF HE HAS A HEART ATTACK WHILE HE'S FLYING THROUGH THE AIR ON CHRISTMAS EVE ?!
© 1985 United Feature Syndicate, Inc.
12-9

LOOK AT THAT PICTURE AGAIN..NOTICE ANYTHING?

LIKE WHAT?
HE DOESN'T HAVE A COPILOT!!
SCHULZ

IS THIS THE LINE TO SEE SANTA CLAUS?
I HOPE SO

HE SURE LOOKS FAT, DOESN'T HE?
© 1985 United Feature Syndicate, Inc.
12-10

WEIGHT LOSS IN PATIENTS WITH A LARGE STOMACH MAY IMPROVE WALKING, AND THUS LEAD TO FEWER ANGINAL ATTACKS

MAYBE I AM IN THE WRONG LINE!
SCHULZ

12-11
HEY, KID..DID YOU EVER THINK ABOUT SANTA CLAUS HAVING A CORONARY?
A WHAT?
See SANTA Today- Hours 1-3

WHEN YOU GET UP THERE TO TALK TO HIM, CHECK HIS EAR LOBES...
DO WHAT?

A DEEP CREASE IN THE EAR LOBES COULD INDICATE CHANGE IN CORONARY VESSELS...
© 1985 United Feature Syndicate, Inc.

CHECK HIS EAR LOBES..
DO WHAT?!
SCHULZ

MR. SANTA CLAUS? MY NAME IS SALLY.. I'M CONCERNED ABOUT YOUR WEIGHT...
12-12

WHEN WAS THE LAST TIME YOU HAD A STRESS TEST? HOW IS YOUR CHOLESTEROL?

DO YOU HAVE A CREASE IN YOUR EAR LOBES?
© 1985 United Feature Syndicate, Inc.

JUST LET ME CHECK THOSE EAR LOBES..
HEY!
SCHULZ

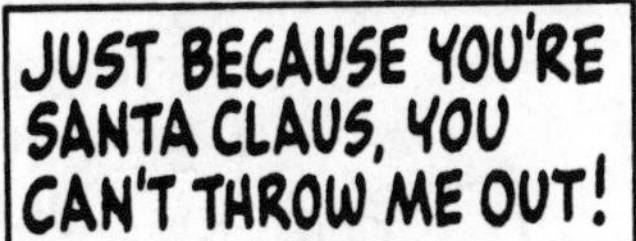

AND YOU HAVE A CREASE IN YOUR EAR LOBE!!

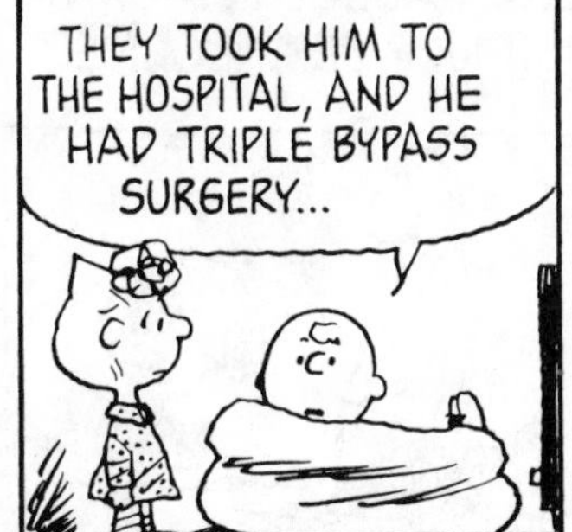

THEY SAID THAT JUST BEFORE HIS HEART ATTACK, THERE WAS SOME KIND OF DISTURBANCE BY A LITTLE GIRL AT THE STORE...

PEANUTS
featuring
"Good ol' Charlie Brown"
by SCHULZ
THIS IS FROM THE SECOND CHAPTER OF LUKE...

"IN THOSE DAYS A DECREE WENT OUT FROM CAESAR AUGUSTUS THAT ALL THE WORLD SHOULD BE ENROLLED"

CAESAR AUGUSTUS WAS THE EMPEROR OF ROME AND THE MOST POWERFUL PERSON ON EARTH!
12-22

ONE NIGHT, IN THE LITTLE TOWN OF BETHLEHEM, A CHILD WAS BORN, BUT NO ONE PAID ANY ATTENTION..AFTER ALL, HE WAS BORN IN A COMMON STABLE...

WHO WOULD HAVE THOUGHT THAT THIS CHILD WOULD SOMEDAY BE REVERED BY MILLIONS WHILE CAESAR AUGUSTUS WOULD BE ALMOST FORGOTTEN ?

NO ONE PAID ANY ATTENTION WHEN I WAS BORN, EITHER, BUT NOW EVERYONE LOVES ME, AND I'M GONNA GET SO MANY PRESENTS FOR CHRISTMAS, IT'LL MAKE YOUR HEAD SWIM!

HEY, AREN'T YOU GONNA FINISH THE STORY ?
I THINK YOU FINISHED IT..

WOW!
© 1985 United Feature Syndicate, Inc.

I THINK THE TEACHER IS TRYING TO TELL ME SOMETHING, MARCIE

WHAT GRADE DID YOU GET, SIR?

AN EXTRA-STRENGTH D MINUS!
12-16

THAT WAS A HARD TEST..HOW'D YOU EVER GET AN "A"?

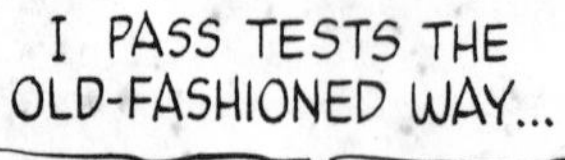

I PASS TESTS THE OLD-FASHIONED WAY...

I STUDY!!
© 1985 United Feature Syndicate, Inc.

12-17
YOU'RE WEIRD, MARCIE!